KU-512-954

MUSLIM
Prayer and Worship

Muhammad Ibrahim and Anita Ganeri

W

FRANKLIN WATTS

LONDON•SYDNEY

First published in 2006 by
Franklin Watts
338 Euston Road
London NW1 3BH

Franklin Watts Australia
Hachette Children's Books
Level 17/207 Kent Street
Sydney NSW2000

Copyright © Franklin Watts 2006

Editor: Rachel Cooke
Design: Joelle Wheelwright

Acknowledgements: Ilyas Dean/Image Works/Topfoto: front cover c, 9.
Bernd Ducke/Superbild/A1 pix: 28. Paul Gapper/World Religions Photo
Library: 27. Gaudard/A1 pix: 17. Ali Haider/epa/Corbis: 25. Zainal Ad
Halim/Reuters/Corbis: 24. Muhammad Ibrahim: 6, 8, 10. Gideon Mendel/
Corbis: 16. Kazuyoshi Nomachi/Corbis: 14. Bernd Obermann/Corbis: 13.
Christine Osborne/World Religions Photo Library: 11, 19, 20, 22, 23, 26, 29.
Helene Rogers/ArkReligion: front cover b, 4, 5. 15. Claire Stout/World
Religions Photo Library: 12. World Religions Photo Library: 7, 18.

Every attempt has been made to clear copyright. Should there be any
inadvertent omission please apply to the publisher for rectification.

A CIP catalogue record for this book is available from the British
Library.

Dewey Decimal Classification Number: 297

ISBN-10: 0-7496-5938-6
ISBN-13: 978-0-7496-5938-7

Printed in China

KINGSTON UPON THAMES PUBLIC LIBRARIES	
07 908180	
ALL NM	CLASS J 200
CAT	REF
P 12-99	06/06

Kingston Libraries

This item can be returned
or renewed at a Kingston
Borough Library on or
before the latest date
stamped below. If the item
is not reserved by another
reader it may be renewed
by telephone up to a
maximum of three times by
quoting your membership
number. Only items issued
for the standard three-week
loan period are renewable.
www.kingston.gov.uk/libraries

Royal
Kingston

New Malden Library
Kingston Road
New Malden
KT3 3LY
Tel: 020 8547 6490

JUNIOR

15. MAY 07	0 9 JAN 2010	2 0 OCT 2015
17. APR 08		2 4 OCT 2016
	2 0 MAR 2010	
31. MAY 08		
04 AUG 08	2 7 FEB 2012	
18. DEC 08		
	0 3 NOV 2012	
31. JAN 09	- 2 NOV 2013	
27 NOV 2009	INVESTOR IN PEOPLE	

KT 0790818 0

Contents

About Islam   4

Muslim Prayer and Worship   6

Set Prayers   8

Worship in the Mosque   10

Prayers from the Qur'an   12

Prayer of Light   14

Prayer for Forgiveness   16

Rules to Live By   18

Family Prayers   20

Prayers for the Birth of a Baby   22

Hajj Prayers   24

Prayers for Id   26

Final Prayers   28

Glossary   30

Further information   31

Index   32

The prayers in this book were chosen by Muhammad Ibrahim, Head of Religious Studies at Southgate School, London. Muhammad is a practising Muslim and has been involved in religious education for many years. He is also a member of the RE Council for England and Wales. The formal prayers in this book have been taken directly from the Qur'an and the Sunnah. Other informal prayers have been adapted from these two sources.

About Islam

Muslims follow the religion of Islam. The word 'Islam' means 'submission' or 'obedience' in the Arabic language. Muslims submit to (obey) the will of God, whom they call Allah, and follow Allah's guidance in all aspects of their lives.

The one true God

Muslims believe that Allah is the one true God who created the world and everything in it. They believe that Islam was the first religion because Allah gave it to Adam, the first man. Adam was the first of many prophets (messengers) chosen by Allah to teach people about Islam. Islam was 'completed' by the last and greatest prophet, the Prophet Muhammad (SAWS) who lived in Saudi Arabia about 1,400 years ago. Allah gave the Qur'an (see page 12) to Muhammad so that Islam could never be changed again.

Showing respect

When mentioning the name of the Prophet Muhammad (SAWS), Muslims should always say immediately afterwards '*Sallallahu alaihi wasallam*' meaning 'Peace and blessings of Allah be upon him'. They do this as a sign of respect. In written texts, the phrase is abbreviated to SAWS.

A Muslim girl prays to Allah for guidance.

4

Muslims around the world

There are about 1.3 billion Muslims in the world, about a quarter of the world's population. They live in many different countries. Indonesia has the largest number of Muslims in the world, followed by India, Pakistan and Bangladesh. About 2 million Muslims live in Britain.

↑ *The Shahadah is often written in Arabic over the entrance*
ⁱ *to a mosque, as here. Arabic reads from right to left.*

The Shahadah

La ilaha illallahu Muhammadur rasulullah

There is no god except Allah; Muhammad is Allah's messenger.

About this prayer

This prayer is called the Shahadah. It states what a Muslim believes. Firstly, it states that there is only one God and no other. At a simple level, in everyday life, this means not treating people like popstars or sports stars, or objects like money, as gods. Secondly, it states that Muhammad (SAWS) is a Prophet of Allah. Someone can become a Muslim by saying and believing in the Shahadah. But they must take their commitment seriously, believe in the Shahadah honestly and try to put it into practice throughout their lives.

Muslim Prayer and Worship

In Arabic, the word for worship is 'Ibadah' which means being in the service of Allah. Muslims believe that Allah calls everyone to worship Him. Ibadah is for Allah alone which is why Muslims should only pray to Allah.

Saying prayers

Prayer is a very important part of a Muslim's daily life. Every good Muslim must perform their prayers five times a day (see right). These set prayers are called 'Salah' (see page 8). It was the angel Jibril who taught Muhammad (SAWS) how to pray. Muslims can also say personal prayers at any time. These are called 'Du'a' and are a way of calling on Allah. The Prophet Muhammad would say Du'a silently or aloud with others, so Muslims do either today. They pray to Allah for help and guidance.

This special clock helps Muslims to work out the times for prayer.

So glory be to Allah,
When you reach the
evening
And when you rise in
the morning:
Yes, to Him be praise,
In the heavens and
on earth;
And in the late
afternoon
And when the day
begins to decline.

About this prayer

These two verses come from the Qur'an (30:17-18). They describe the times at which a Muslim should pray their Salah. Muslims pray because Allah has told them to and because they gain great benefit from it. They pray as if they are standing in the presence of Allah.

The five set prayer times are:

1) Fajr: Early in the morning at dawn.

2) Zuhr: At midday when the sun has just passed its highest point.

3) Asr: In mid-afternoon when your shadow is the same length as your body.

4) Magrib: Just after sunset.

5) Isha: After sunset and before midnight.

The Hadith

Muslims sometimes like to say the same prayers as Muhammad (SAWS). These can be found in books, called the Hadith, which contain the sayings of Muhammad (SAWS) (see page 15).

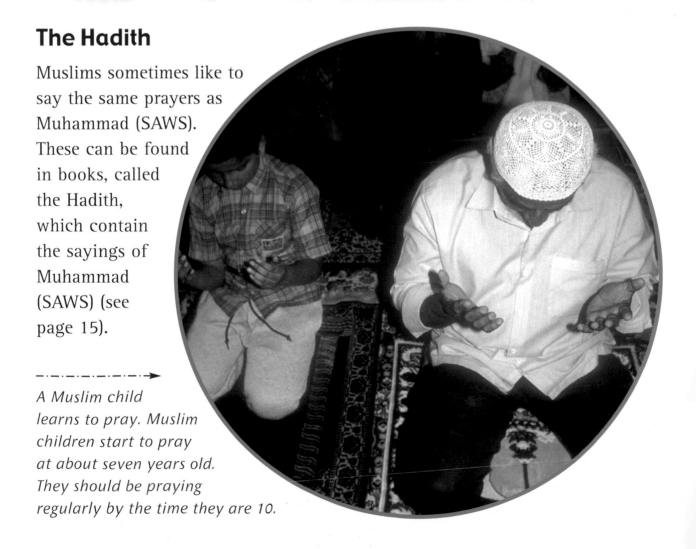

A Muslim child learns to pray. Muslim children start to pray at about seven years old. They should be praying regularly by the time they are 10.

Set Prayers

The set prayers which Muslims say five times a day are called 'Salah'. The word 'Salah' comes from the Arabic for 'to communicate'. By saying their prayers, Muslims believe that they are communicating directly with Allah.

Five Pillars of Islam

Salah is the second of the Five Pillars of Islam. These are five duties which help Muslims to put their beliefs into practice. Carrying out the Five Pillars shows that Muslims are putting their faith above everything else in their lives. The Five Pillars are:

1 The Shahadah: declaration of faith (see page 5)
2 Salah: five daily prayers
3 Zakah: money paid to help others
4 Sawm: fasting in the month of Ramadan (see page 26)
5 Hajj: pilgrimage to Makkah (see page 24).

For Wudu, Muslims wash their face, hands and feet and also wipe their heads.

Preparing for prayer

Before Salah, Muslims must prepare themselves for prayer. They must put aside all other thoughts and concentrate on Allah. If they do not, their prayers will not be worthwhile. They must also wear clean clothes and wash themselves in a special way. This washing is called 'Wudu' and it is part of the act of worship. Wudu helps to make the worshipper clean in both body and mind.

Words and movements

As Muslims say the words of the prayers, they perform a series of set movements. Each set of movements is called a rak'ah. There is a set number of rak'ahs for each time of prayer. These words and movements were taught by the Prophet Muhammad (SAWS) to the first Muslims and have not changed since that time. They are copied by all Muslims all over the world. The panel below shows a selection of movements and words made and said when Muslims pray their Salah.

1 *Qiyam.* Muslims stand upright with both hands raised up to their ears. They recite 'Allahu Akbar' which means 'God is the Greatest'. They place their left hands on their chests with their right hands on top. Then they recite certain verses from the Qur'an.

2 *Ruku.* Muslims bow at the waist and place their hands on their knees. They say: 'Sami' allahu liman hamidah', meaning 'Our Lord, praise be to You'.

3 *Sujud.* This is when Muslims kneel with their hands and faces on the ground. Seven parts of the body should touch the ground (two sets of toes, two knees, two hands and the face). In this position, the Muslim says: 'Subhana rabbiyal a'la' which means 'Glory to my Lord, the Highest'.

A group of Muslims pray together. They are at different stages of their Salah.

4 At the end of Salah, Muslims rise to a kneeling position with their hands on their knees. They turn their heads first to the right, then to the left, and offer the person on either side this greeting: 'Assalamu alaikum wa rahmatullah' which means 'Peace and the Mercy of Allah be upon you'.

9

Worship in the Mosque

A Muslim place for prayer is called a mosque. The Arabic word for mosque is 'masjid'. Mosques are usually thought of as buildings where Muslims can come together to pray. But anywhere that a Muslim chooses for prayer is believed to become a mosque for that particular time.

Mosques need not take on any specific shape or form. Some are purpose-built, like this one in Palmer's Green, London, that is almost complete. Others are converted from other buildings.

Call to prayer

Muslim daily prayers start with the call to prayer which is given from the minaret of the mosque. This is called the 'Adhan' (see page 23). The call to prayer is given by a person called a 'Mu'adhin'. Traditionally, a Mu'adhin would call from a minaret tower, but today, in some countries, he can be heard through a loudspeaker. Muslim women are not expected to go to the mosque, although they can if they wish to. They usually say their prayers at home. Muslim men should attend the mosque at least once a week for midday prayers on Fridays.

Friday prayers

Fridays are special days to Muslims. They believe that Allah created Adam, the first man, on a Friday. This makes Fridays a time for Muslims to remember the precious gift of life that Allah has given. Midday prayers on Fridays are called 'Jumu'ah' which means 'gathering'. If possible, all Muslim men try to attend the mosque. They believe that praying with others in the mosque will bring greater blessings and help to build up a stronger community spirit.

When Muslims pray, they must turn to face the Ka'bah in Makkah in Saudi Arabia. This direction is called 'qiblah'. In many mosques, the qiblah wall is marked by a qiblah arch.

O you who believe,
When you hear the call
to prayer on Friday.
Go quickly to remember Allah.
Leave your business
(or what you are doing)
That is best for you, if you but knew.

And when the Prayer is finished,
You can go back through the land,
Seek the goodness of Allah,
And remember Allah often so that
you may do well.

About this prayer

These verses come from the Qur'an (62:9-10). They tell Muslims that when they hear the call to prayer on Friday, they must go to the mosque and remember Allah. Afterwards, they should remember Allah when they go back to their daily tasks. On a Friday, the midday prayer called 'Zuhr' is replaced with the Jumu'ah prayer, which will include a talk by the Imam. He is a senior person who leads the prayers in the mosque. The talk helps to remind people of their duties as good Muslims.

Prayers from the Qur'an

Many of the prayers used in Muslim worship come from the Qur'an. This is the sacred book of the Muslims. They believe that the Qur'an is the direct word of Allah and treat it with great respect. They believe that the Qur'an was revealed in Arabic as a guide to help Muslims live their lives properly.

Reading aloud

Muslims should not simply read the Qur'an but should try to put its teachings into practice. In Arabic, the word 'Qur'an' means 'to read out loud'. That is why, as part of Muslim prayer, verses from the Qur'an are often recited out loud. Even if listeners do not understand every word, they may be inspired by hearing them.

Two Muslim boys in Kenya read from the Qur'an. The script is Arabic.

The Qur'an

Muslims believe that Allah gave the verses of the Qur'an to the Prophet Muhammad (SAWS) over many years. Muhammad could not read or write but memorised the words. He also recited them to his companions who learned them by heart. After Muhammad's death, they collected all the verses together and wrote them down in one book. The verses were not changed in any way and have not been changed since.

↑ A Qari recites from the Qur'an at a mosque. A Qari is a hafiz (someone who has learnt the Qur'an by heart).

In the name of Allah, the Kindest and Most Merciful.
Praise is for Allah, Master of the Universe,
The Kindest and Most Merciful One,
King of the Day of Judgement.
You are the One we worship;
You are the One we ask for help.
Show us the straight path;
The path of those whom You are pleased with,
Not the path of those who deserve Your anger,
Nor those who become lost.

About this prayer

The Qur'an is divided into 114 surahs (chapters), made up of 6,616 ayats (verses). These are the first verses of the Qur'an (1: 1-7). They are called 'Al-Fatihah' ('The Opening') and are a prayer to Allah for guidance. The rest of the Qur'an is the answer to this prayer. Muslims recite these verses during each rak'ah of their Salah so they say them many times a day. The verses express the Muslim belief that Allah is the only one they should worship. They also ask Allah for help and guidance in living their life in a way that pleases Him.

Prayer of Light

Muslims believe that the Qur'an is the word of Allah. But it can only make sense if we can understand it. People have different experiences in different times and places. To understand the Qur'an, it is important to try to understand what it was like for people living at the time of the Prophet Muhammad (SAWS).

The city of Makkah where Muhammad was born.

The life of the Prophet

The Prophet Muhammad (SAWS) lived from 570-632CE in the country we now call Saudi Arabia. Muslims try hard to follow the example of what he said and how he lived. This example is known as the 'Sunnah' and it is written down in the Hadith (see next page). It is a rich and valuable source of prayers and inspiration for Muslims. For example, if Muslims have a problem, they turn to the Sunnah or the Qur'an to see what Muhammad might have done in a similar situation. This might mean trying to find a rule to deal with a modern activity, such as smoking. Muslims are not allowed to smoke because smoking can kill you and the Sunnah shows that it is wrong to kill yourself.

14

O Allah, place light in my heart, and on my tongue light, and in my ears light and in my sight light, and above me light, and below me light, and to my right light and behind me light. Place in my soul light. Magnify for me light, and amplify for me light. Make for me light and make me a light. O Allah, grant me light, and place light in my nerves, and in my body light and in my blood light and in my hair light and in my skin light. O Allah, make for me a light in my grave... and a light in my bones. Increase me in light, increase in me light, increase in me light. Grant me light upon light.

About this prayer

The words of this prayer are part of the Sunnah. They come from books called the Hadith, which are collections of the Prophet Muhammad (SAWS)'s sayings and accounts of his actions. They were put together after Muhammad's death to report the Sunnah and record what reliable people remembered of Muhammad's life. This prayer talks about light or truth which is an important symbol of hope and inspiration. Muslims may either think or recite it when they pray their Du'a (private prayers to Allah).

This is a shortened volume of a collection of Hadith made by Sahih Al-Bukhari.

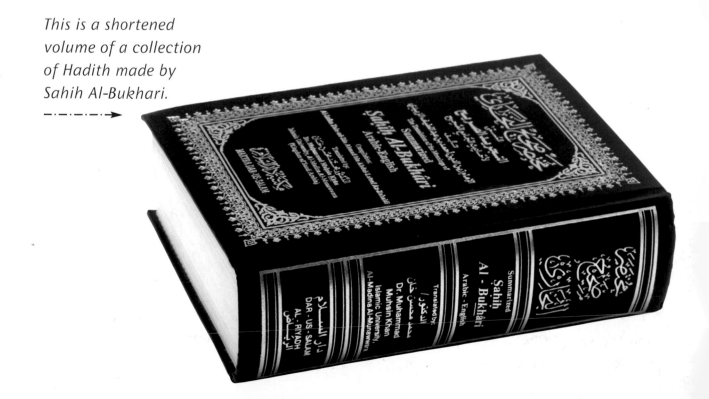

Prayer for Forgiveness

Everyone makes mistakes and does things that they regret. But Muslims believe that Allah will forgive anyone who is genuinely sorry for what they have done and who promises to try to do better in future. Forgiveness is a very important quality in Islam.

Thinking of others

Islam teaches that when we do good things, it not only helps ourselves but also others. Similarly doing bad things can hurt many people. We must make the effort to say sorry and encourage others to make the effort to forgive us.

A group of children play together. Even when you play, you need to think of others.

The names of Allah

In Arabic, one of the names for Allah is 'Al Ghaffar' which means 'the Great Forgiver'. Muslims believe that Allah has many names. Each of them tells us about one of Allah's qualities. For example, Allah may be called 'Ar Rahman' which means 'the Most Compassionate', or 'Al Karim' which means 'the Generous One'. Trying to develop these qualities, and to be more compassionate or generous, will help us to live our lives in a better way and to make the world a better place.

A Muslim girl says a private prayer (Du'a). She may include the prayer below.

'To make things easy'

Do not punish us if we do things that are wrong because of forgetfulness or because we do not know that they are wrong. Please do not make things as difficult for us as you have done to those before us. Help us to cope with those things we find too difficult. Forgive us when we do those things that are wrong. We know you are looking after us. Help us to help those who do not understand this.

About this prayer

This prayer is adapted from the Qur'an (2:286). It may be said at anytime when Muslims pray their Du'a. The Qur'anic verse itself may be recited as part of Salah after the Al-Fatihah. Often this verse is written on cards for Muslims to read whenever they feel worried, when things have gone wrong or someone has died. It helps to give them comfort so that they can cope. It asks Allah to help us in difficult times and to forgive us if we do something wrong.

17

Rules to Live By

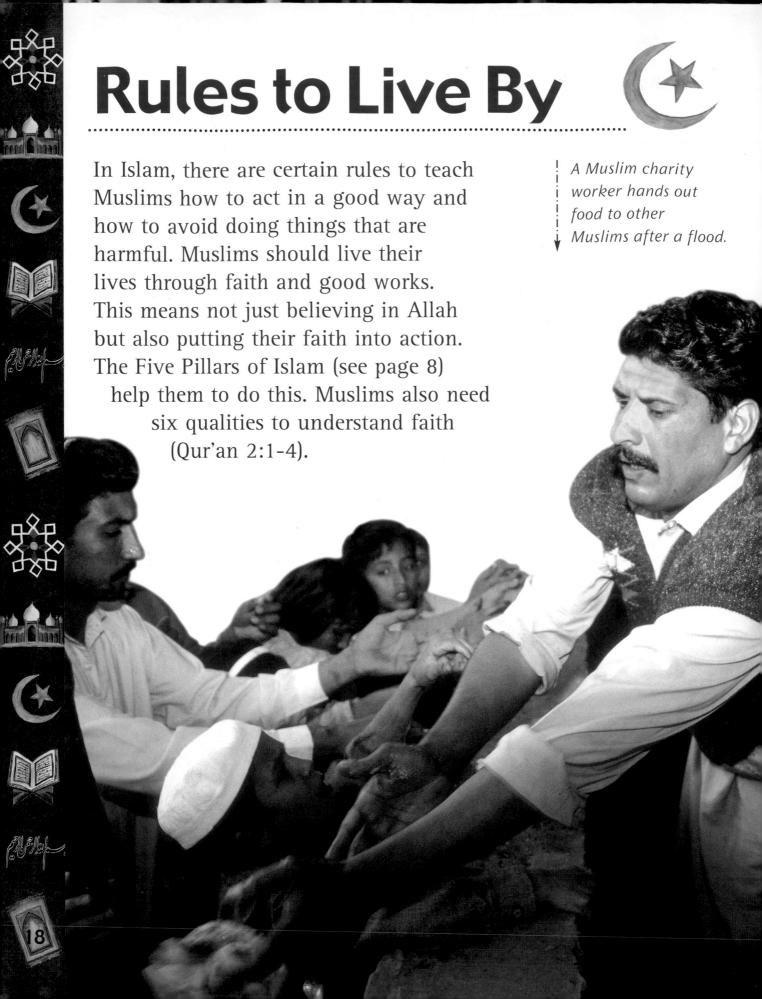

In Islam, there are certain rules to teach Muslims how to act in a good way and how to avoid doing things that are harmful. Muslims should live their lives through faith and good works. This means not just believing in Allah but also putting their faith into action. The Five Pillars of Islam (see page 8) help them to do this. Muslims also need six qualities to understand faith (Qur'an 2:1-4).

A Muslim charity worker hands out food to other Muslims after a flood.

Six Qualities for Faith

1 **Piety** – knowing how to live as a good, kind person.

2 **Ghayb** – believing in things beyond our understanding, such as Allah, paradise and angels.

3 **Salah** – being able to pray five times a day, every day.

4 **Giving freely** – believing that your life is not your own, to do as you please, but seeing it as a loan from Allah and using it responsibly to please Allah and help others.

5 **Revelations** – Allah has given guidance to humans to help them to know what is right and wrong. Books like the Qur'an are examples of such guidance.

6 **Akhirah** – believing in a life after death.

O Allah, I pray that I can listen to and be obedient to your guidance,
So that through my bad or thoughtless behaviour I may not encourage others to do the same.
Or that I too may not be misguided by them,
Or that I cause others to avoid doing good things,
Or they cause me to do harm,
Or that I abuse other people,
Or that they abuse me,
Or that I behave foolishly
Or indeed meet the foolishness of their behaviour.
Help me to encourage others to do good things,
So that they can encourage me to do good things,
So that I can be kind to others,
So that they will be kind to me,
So that I can behave with thought and care,
So that they can meet my behaviour with thought and care,
Help me to encourage others not to do silly things.

About this prayer

Muslims use the teachings of the Qur'an and the Sunnah as guides for living their lives. This prayer is taken from the Hadith. It could be said as a private prayer by someone leaving home to go to school or work and asking for Allah's guidance in the day ahead. It reminds Muslims to be kind and helpful to others, and to set a good example by their own good deeds.

Family Prayers

Family life is an important part of Islam. It is vital to look after our families because then society will look after itself. A large part of this belief is showing love and respect to our parents and teachers because they will be the ones teaching us to become caring, kind and wise.

The Ummah

Muslims are asked to consider their actions carefully. They are not just responsible for their own actions but for the effect of their actions on the whole community. In Islam, the community is known as the 'Ummah' which means the worldwide family of Muslims.

A Muslim family gathers for a meal.

Praying together

Since Salah has set prayers, it means that millions of Muslims across the world say the same prayers every day. This helps Muslims to feel part of a much wider family as well as their own.

------------------>

In Islam an elderly man is given the title 'Sheik' to mean someone who is wise and learned.

'To respect my parents and my teachers'
Help me to learn not to be so selfish and to think carefully about why my parents and my teachers want me to do well.
Help me to be kind to my parents and to those who care for me.
Help me to want to care for my parents when they get old.
Encourage me not to say anything that will make them angry.
Encourage me not to say bad things to them, nor to shout at them.
Encourage me to speak to them softly with kind words of honour and respect.

Encourage me to be humble and kind when they are angry with me, as I know they love me and want me to do well.

About this prayer

This prayer is adapted from a selection of verses from the Qur'an and the Hadith. It may be said as a private prayer. Muslim children are encouraged to think carefully about those who are older than them. Parents and teachers should speak with respect and set a good example to those who are in their care. In turn, children should show love and respect to their elders. They should not answer back or disobey people who are trying to help them. They should honour their parents and care for them in old age.

Prayers for the Birth of a Baby

For Muslims, a baby is a gift from Allah and parents have a special responsibility to look after their children. From an early age, parents teach their children to be good Muslims, to learn about their faith and to work hard and care for others.

A father whispers the Adhan (see opposite) into his new-born baby's ear.

Choosing a name

When a baby is born, a ceremony called 'Aqiqah' is held to give the child its name. Muslims believe that it is important to give children a name with a good meaning. Many Muslim boys are named after the Prophet Muhammad (SAWS). Others are given one of the names of Allah, such as Hafiz (Protector) or Karim (Generous). 'Abdul', meaning servant, is added in front of these names because it is wrong to call someone 'Allah'. So the name 'Abdul Hafiz' means 'Servant of the Protector'. Many Muslim girls are named after famous early Muslim women who were followers of Muhammad or members of his family.

Allah is the Greatest, Allah is the Greatest,
Allah is the Greatest, Allah is the Greatest,
I bear witness that there
is no god but Allah,
I bear witness that there
is no god but Allah,
I bear witness that Muhammad
is Allah's messenger,
I bear witness that Muhammad
is Allah's messenger,
Rush to prayer, Rush to prayer,
Rush to success, Rush to success,
Allah is the Greatest,
Allah is the Greatest.

About this prayer
This prayer is called the Adhan (the call to prayer). It is called out from the mosque in Arabic before every Salah. It is also said when a Muslim baby is born. The father whispers the Adhan into the baby's right ear so that the first word the baby is likely to hear will be 'Allah'. Just as the Adhan calls Muslims to prayer, it also calls the baby to a life of prayer and devotion to Allah.

↑ *A Mu'adhin standing in a minaret tower calls people to prayer with the Adhan.*

Hajj Prayers

Once a year, over two million Muslims gather in and around the city of Makkah in Saudi Arabia to celebrate the pilgrimage called Hajj. Hajj is one of the Five Pillars of Islam and all Muslims try to make Hajj at least once in their lifetimes. Muslims believe that the first time they perform Hajj, all of their sins are washed away. Hajj gives Muslims a chance for a fresh start.

Here I am at Your service, O Allah
You have no partner
Here I am at Your service, O Allah
Verily, all the praise, the grace belong to You,
And the kingdom.
You have no partner.

About this prayer

This prayer is recited by Muslims many times during Hajj. It is called 'Talbiyah' which means 'to follow' or 'to obey'. It is one of the prayers said by the Prophet Muhammad (SAWS) when he was performing Hajj. Muslims start reciting this prayer when they reach the Ka'bah in the centre of the great mosque in Makkah. The Ka'bah is the most important building in Islam and Muslims turn to face it when they pray.

Muslims walking and praying around the Ka'bah in Makkah.

24

The route of Hajj

When pilgrims arrive in Makkah, they walk around the Ka'bah seven times. Then they walk or run between two nearby hills and visit the well of Zamzam. This reminds them of the story of Hajar (the wife of the Prophet Ibrahim) who had to search in the desert for water for her son. Later, the pilgrims gather on the Plain of Arafat where the Prophet Muhammad (SAWS) gave his last sermon. This is the main part of Hajj. Here the pilgrims stand and pray for forgiveness for their sins. After this, at a place called Mina, they throw stones at three pillars which stand for the devil.

Pilgrims dressed in ihram pray on the Plain of Arafat.

Pilgrims' dress

During Hajj, pilgrims wear special clothes called 'ihram'. All men wear two plain white sheets of cloth. One is worn around the waist; the other around the shoulders. There is no set dress for women. They wear their ordinary, modest clothes. Wearing similar clothes shows that everyone is equal in Allah's eyes. This is important for Muslims. They believe that, on the Day of Judgement, Allah will judge everyone on their good or bad deeds, not on whether they are rich or poor. Allah teaches that everyone is equal apart from those who do a greater number of good deeds.

Prayers for Id

The two main festivals in Islam are Id-ul-Fitr and Id-ul-Adha. The Prophet Muhammad (SAWS) spoke of Id-ul-Adha as being the more important of the two. The word 'Id' means 'feast' or 'celebration'. These two festivals are especially happy times when Muslims celebrate their faith and give thanks to Allah.

A Muslim makes an Id gift of money called 'Zakat-ul-Fitr'.

Id-ul-Adha

The festival of Id-ul-Adha takes place at the end of the Hajj pilgrimage. Its name means 'festival of the sacrifice'. At this time, Muslims remember the story of how the Prophet Ibrahim was ready to kill his son, Isma'il, to show his willingness to obey Allah. Allah told Ibrahim that he had proved his love and gave him a ram to sacrifice instead. Today, Muslims still sacrifice a sheep or goat. Some of the meat is shared out among family and friends. Some is given to the poor so that they too can enjoy an Id feast.

Id-ul-Fitr

Id-ul-Fitr marks the end of Ramadan, the month of fasting. During this time, Muslims do not eat or drink during the hours of daylight. They will only eat after sunset and before it starts to get light in the morning. Id-ul-Fitr is a time when Muslims work hard to make their community better and stronger. To help bring this about, they make a special gift of money to Muslims who are poor and needy.

*When we are down, or upset,
we sometimes do things because
we are angry.
When we are up, or happy, we
sometimes do things because we
want to share our happiness.
We often do things to tell others
how we feel.
A nasty stare or frown will tell
others we are unhappy.
A gentle kiss or a smiling face will
show we are happy.
A kiss or a smile is one of the greatest
gifts we can give in charity.
All of this will amount to nothing
unless we strive to have a good
heart.
We should strive to please others
because we want to please them.
We should strive to please God
because we want to please Him.
We should try to be genuine, honest
and sincere in all that we do.*

About this prayer

On Id morning, Muslims go to the
mosque for Id prayers. They pray two
rak'ahs, then listen to a talk given by the
Imam. Afterwards, they visit relatives,
friends and neighbours to exchange gifts
and wish them a happy Id. Id is a time
of happiness for everyone to share.
The prayer above is one which Muslims
might say in private after Salah at Id.
Its message is that our good deeds mean
nothing unless we mean them sincerely.

*Muslims celebrate Id by exchanging
gifts with their family and friends.*

Final Prayers

The first word a Muslim baby should hear is 'Allah' (see pages 22-23). When a Muslim is dying, he or she should try to say the Shahadah (see page 5) so that the last word he or she says is also 'Allah'. When a Muslim hears of the death of someone they should say: '*To Allah we belong, and to Him we return.*' In this way, Allah should be at the heart of a Muslim's life from its beginning to its end.

The Islamic gardens of the Alhambra Palace in Spain. Muslims believe paradise (see next page) to be like a beautiful garden.

28

Day of Judgement

Muslims believe that on the Day of Judgement, they can hope to be reunited with their loved ones. This gives great comfort to a dying person and to their loved ones. On the Day of Judgement, Allah will judge everyone according to how they have lived. Good people will be rewarded with paradise. Wicked people will be punished in hell. Muslims must remember that paradise is not given automatically. It has to be worked for. They also know that Allah is a good and merciful judge, ready to forgive people if they are truly sorry for their wrong-doings.

↑ *A Muslim recites prayers at a grave.*

The Funeral Prayers

Salah is prayed without full prostrations.
The following Du'a may be said:
*O Allah forgive us, both those who are alive and those who have died;
Those who are near to us and those who are far away;
Keep those of us who are here to always remain true to Your will;
Keep those who are dying firm and strong in their faith.*

As the body is lowered into the ground, the following is said:
In the name of Allah, we commit you to this earth, according to the Way of the Prophet of Allah.

About this prayer

These are a selection of the prayers recited at a Muslim's funeral. Muslims have to be buried, not cremated. This is because Muslims believe that their bodies will lie in the grave until the Day of Judgement. They are buried facing towards the city of Makkah. The final prayers are called 'Salat ul Janaza' which means 'funeral prayers'. These are the same words as the daily Salah but Muslims do not prostrate themselves on the ground. Being aware of death helps Muslims to focus on what life is for, that is to gain Allah's blessing.

29

Glossary

Adhan The words of the call to prayer made from the mosque before each prayer time. They are also whispered into a new-born baby's ear.

Al-Fatihah The first, or opening, chapter of the Qur'an.

Allah The Islamic name for God in the Arabic language.

Arabic The religious language of Islam. The Qur'an is written in Arabic and Muslims pray in Arabic.

Du'a Personal prayers said by Muslims. The word 'Du'a' means 'call' or 'summon' and these prayers are a way of calling on Allah.

Hadith The sayings and actions of the Prophet Muhammad (SAWS). These were reported by people who knew him and written down later.

Hafiz The title given to someone who has learnt the Qur'an off by heart.

Hajj The annual pilgrimage to Makkah, one of the Five Pillars of Islam.

Ibadah The Arabic word for all acts of worship. It means any actions performed in the service of Allah, including prayers.

Id The Arabic for festival or holiday.

Imam A person who leads prayers in the mosque and gives a talk at Friday midday prayers.

Islam The religion given by Allah for humans to follow, in order to gain peace. Followers of Islam are called Muslims.

Jumu'ah The weekly prayers performed by Muslims in the mosque shortly after midday on a Friday. The word 'Jumu'ah' means 'to collect' or 'unite'.

Ka'bah The cube-shaped building in the centre of the grand mosque in Makkah. It is the holiest building in Islam. Muslims turn to face it when they say their prayers.

Makkah The city where the Prophet Muhammad (SAWS) was born and where the Ka'bah is found. Muslims visit Makkah to perform the Hajj pilgrimage.

Minaret A tower attached to a mosque from which the Adhan is given.

Mosque A place of Muslim prayer. The Arabic word for mosque is 'masjid' which means a place of prostration (bowing down before Allah).

Mu'adhin The person who gives the call to prayer. It is sometimes spelt Muezzin.

Prophets Special people chosen by Allah to act as His messengers and to teach people about His wishes.

Qur'an The holy book of Islam revealed (given) to the Prophet Muhammad (SAWS) by Allah.

Rak'ah A unit of the set words and movements of Salah prayer.

Ramadan The month of fasting in the Islamic calendar.

Salah The formal prayers which Muslims perform five times a day.

SAWS Short for 'Sallallahu alaihi wasallam' meaning 'Peace and blessings of Allah be upon him'. Muslims should always say this immediately after mentioning Muhammad (SAWS) by name.

Shahadah The declaration of faith. It sums up what Muslims believe about Allah and about Muhammad (SAWS).

Sunnah The words, actions and customs of the Prophet Muhammad (SAWS). These are written down in the Hadith. Muslims use them as a guide for their lives and worship.

Further information

Books to read
Sacred Texts: The Qur'an
Anita Ganeri, Evans Brothers 2003

Muslim Festivals Through the Year
Anita Ganeri, Franklin Watts 2003

Religion in Focus: Islam
Geoff Teece, Franklin Watts 2003

Keystones: Muslim Mosque
Umar Hegedus, A & C Black 2000

World Religions: Islam
Richard Tames, Franklin Watts 1999

Websites
www.mcb.org.uk
The website of the Muslim Council of Britain.

www.islamic-foundation.org.uk
The Islamic Foundation's website, including additional resources.

www.iqratrust.org
Website of Iqra Trust, a Muslim educational charity.

www.islamic-relief.org.uk
Website of Islamic Relief, an international aid organisation.

Index

Adhan 10, 22, 23, 30
Akhirah 19
Al-Fatihah 13, 17, 30
Allah 4, 5, 6, 7 *and throughout*
Arabic 4, 5, 6, 8, 10, 12, 17, 23, 30

ceremonies,
    baby naming 22, 23
    death 28
    funeral 29
children 7, 16, 17, 21, 22, 28

Day of Judgement 13, 25, 29
Du'a *see* prayers, Du'a

festivals 26-27, 30
Five Pillars of Islam 8, 18, 24, 30

Ghayb 19

Hadith 7, 15, 19, 21, 30, 31
Hajj 8, 24-25, 26, 30
Hazif 13, 30

Ibrahim, Prophet 25, 26

Id-ul-Adha 26-27, 30
Id-ul-Fitr 26-27, 30
ihram 25
Imam 11, 27, 30
Islam
    beginnings 4-5, 14
    beliefs 4, 5, 6, 8, 11, 13, 14, 16-24, 28, 29, 31
    family life 20-21
    teachings 12, 16-21, 25
    ways of worship 5-13, 24, 25, 26, 27, 29

Jumu'ah 11, 30

Ka'bah 11, 24, 25, 30

Makkah 8, 11, 14, 24, 25, 29, 30
minaret 10, 23, 30
mosque 5, 10, 11, 13, 23, 24, 27, 30
Mu'adhin 10, 23, 31
Muhammad (SAWS), Prophet 4, 5, 6, 7, 9, 13, 14, 15, 22, 23, 24, 25, 26, 30, 31

paradise 28, 29
piety 19
pilgrimage 8, 24-25, 26, 30

prayer 5-15, 17, 19, 21, 23, 24, 27, 29, 30, 31
prayers,
    Du'a 6, 15, 17, 29, 30
    Friday 10, 11, 30
    Salah 6, 7, 8, 9, 13, 17, 19, 21, 23, 27, 29, 31
    set 6, 7, 8, 9, 19
prophet 4, 5, 25, 26, 31

Qiyam 9
Qur'an 4, 7, 9, 11, 12, 13, 14, 17, 19, 21, 30, 31

rak'ah 9, 13, 27, 31
Ramadan 8, 26, 31
Revelations 19
Ruku 9

Salah *see* prayers, Salah
Saudi Arabia 4, 11, 14, 24
Sawm 8
Shahadah 5, 8, 28, 31
Six Qualities for Faith 18-19
sujud 9
Sunnah 14, 15, 19, 31

Ummah 20

Wudu 8

32

GODS AND GODDESSES
OF
ANCIENT ROME

LEON ASHWORTH

CHERRYTREE BOOKS

KT-440-803

A Cherrytree Book

Designed and produced by
A S Publishing

First published 2001
by Cherrytree Press
327 High Street
Slough
Berkshire
SL1 1TX

© Evans Brothers Limited 2001

British Library Cataloguing in Publication Data

Ashworth, Leon
    Gods and goddesses of ancient Rome
    1.Gods, Roman – Juvenile literature
    2.Goddesses, Roman – Juvenile literature
    3.Mythology, Roman – Juvenile literature
    4.Rome – Religion – Juvenile literature
    I.Title II.Ancient Rome
    292.2'11

ISBN 1 84234 040 9

Printed in Hong Kong by Wing King Tong Co. Ltd

All rights reserved. No part of this publication may be
reproduced, stored in a retrieval system or transmitted in any
form or by any means, electronic, mechanical, photocopying
or otherwise, without the prior permission of the publishers.

Acknowledgments
Design: Richard Rowan
Artwork: Gwen Green
Consultant: Peter A Clayton FSA
Photographs: *AKG London*: Cover and pages 1, 3, 4 left, 6/7 top &
bottom, 8 bottom left, 9, 10 bottom left, 10/11 top, 12, 13, 14, 15,
16 bottom right, 17, 18 bottom left, 18/19 top, 20, 21, 22, 23
bottom, 24 centre, 24/25 bottom, 26 bottom left, 27,
28, 29; *Peter Clayton*: 2, 4 top, 4/5 bottom, 7 top
right, 8 top left & bottom right, 10 top &
bottom right, 16 bottom left, 18 bottom
right, 19 bottom, 23 top, 24 top, 26 bottom
right; *Werner Forman Archive: 11.*

J292
Ashworth, Leon
Ancient Rome

BL   C407719917
        9.99

21/10/03

C407719917

CONTENTS

ANCIENT ROME   4

ROMAN RELIGION   6

GODS OF THE CITY   8

GODS OF THE HOME   10

JUPITER AND JUNO   12

NEPTUNE, GOD OF THE SEA   14

PLUTO AND THE UNDERWORLD   16

MARS AND VULCAN   18

APOLLO AND DIANA   20

MERCURY AND MINERVA   22

VENUS AND CUPID   24

CERES AND COUNTRY GODS   26

BACCHUS AND HIS REVELS   28

GLOSSARY   30

INDEX   32

ANCIENT ROME

T HE STORY of Rome and its gods began over two thousand years ago, in 753 BC, when the city of Rome is said to have been founded. The city grew up around seven hills alongside the river Tiber in central Italy (see map page 31). Being on a river, the place was good for farming and for trade. The people became rich and powerful, taking over neighbouring cities and governing them well. With their fine army, the Romans went on to conquer the rest of Italy and in time most of Europe and beyond.

ROMULUS AND REMUS

According to legend, Romulus and Remus were twin sons of the god Mars. Their mother's wicked uncle set the babies adrift on the river Tiber in a basket. They were saved from death by a she-wolf who looked after them as her own. The boys were later found by a herdsman who brought them up. As young men they founded the city of Rome. But the two quarrelled and Romulus killed Remus. The surviving twin gave his name to the city. This coin shows the she-wolf suckling the twins.

ADOPTED GODS

In ancient times, only the Jews worshipped a single god. Other ancient peoples, including the Romans, worshipped many gods. They believed that the gods controlled every part of their lives. If you needed help, it was important to know the right god to ask for it. The gods did not always behave well. They carried on in what most people today would regard as a quite ungodly way.

As the Romans conquered new lands and peoples, they gathered new gods and

◀ The Romans made statues of their gods and goddesses, many of which have survived unharmed. Unfortunately this statue of the goddess Minerva has lost its arm.

FAMILY OF THE ROMAN GODS

SATURN
father of the gods

NEPTUNE
god of the sea

VESTA
goddess of fire and the hearth

JUPITER
supreme god and god of the sky

=

JUNO
mother goddess

CERES
goddess of crops

PLUTO
god of the underworld

MERCURY
winged messenger of the gods

MINERVA
goddess of wisdom

BACCHUS
god of wine

APOLLO
god of the sun

DIANA
goddess of the moon

VULCAN
god of fire and forge

=

VENUS
goddess of love

−

MARS
god of war

CUPID
god of love

▲ The Roman gods were descended from Saturn. There were 12 great gods – Jupiter, Juno, Vesta, Minerva, Ceres, Diana, Venus, Mars, Mercury, Neptune, Vulcan, and Apollo. The family tree shows the relationships, some official (=), some not, between the gods.

= MARRIAGE

◀ Rome had many temples. This is the temple of Saturn. Little of the building now remains but Saturn lives on in our name for Saturday.

goddesses. They let conquered people worship their own gods, so long as they also worshipped Roman ones. Many of these gods were simply Greek gods with a different name (see page 31). People in different places told different stories about the gods, but that did not matter.

Eventually, led by the emperor Constantine, the Romans gave up their gods and came to believe in a single god. They adopted the Christian religion.

ROMAN RELIGION

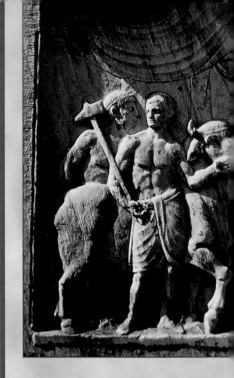

RELIGION WAS part of everyday life. People had shrines in their homes and visited temples. The rulers of Rome made no decisions without consulting priests. Farmers planted crops only when the gods wished them to and army commanders relied on the gods for aid in battle.

Roman religion was about the family first, and then about the state – the 'family of Rome'. In most homes, the family said prayers every day and their main meal was itself a religious ceremony.

PRIESTS AND AUGURS

Festivals and religious ceremonies were run by priests. They kept traditions, followed the rules and recorded important events. Priests were helped by soothsayers, or augurs. These wise men could tell what the gods wanted. They 'read' signs in the sky, such as thunderstorms, clouds, lightning and the flights of birds. They examined the entrails (insides) of sacrificed

RITUAL SACRIFICE

Rituals were held outside the temple on a marble altar. People might bring a chicken, a sheep or even a bull to be sacrificed. Priests and their helpers would hang garlands of flowers round the animal's

VISITING THE TEMPLE

Roman temples usually housed a large statue of the god lit by flickering oil lamps. Individuals would stand before the statue to make their requests for help and place an offering of money or a small statue on the ground. Some might leave a curse against an enemy. There were no religious services inside the temple for people to attend.

allowed to mix with boys or to marry. The innermost sanctuary of Vesta's temple was opened once a year to mothers who visited it barefoot with gifts of food.

His temple gates were open only in time of war – which was most of the time – until the emperors Augustus and Nero brought a few periods of peace to the empire.

The Romans gave Janus credit for starting most things. He was the god of daybreak, and our month of January (the opening of the year) is named after him. He was also the god of departure and return, and Romans relied on him as they navigated their ships in and out of harbours.

▲ The remains of the Forum, the main meeting place in ancient Rome. Today it is a ruin (above), but in Roman times it was full of activity and the bustle of daily life (below).

GODS OF THE HOME

THE ROMANS believed that certain gods looked after their homes and possessions. Every family hearth had a shrine with a statue of Vesta and lesser household gods called Lares and Penates. Vesta presided over the preparation and eating of meals.

Every day the family made offerings to their gods, portions of the family meal, dishes of special cakes, honey, wine and incense. The Penates made sure the family had enough food and drink. They protected the entire household but took particular care of the storeroom. When a family moved, so did the spirits who watched over the household. It was easy to carry their small statues to the new home.

▲ This little statue is a Lar, holding a platter and a loaf of bread. The family said a prayer to their Lar each morning and made special offerings to him at weddings and other family celebrations.

GUARDIANS AND GUIDES

Every boy and girl had a personal spirit to watch over them and shape their character and personality. Boys had a Genius, girls had a Juno. These spirits had various helpers – one made the baby cry for the first time, another taught it to eat and drink, two more taught it to walk, and so on.

◀ Babies were carefully watched over, with a separate god to oversee every aspect of an infant's life.

▲ All the children of the family were taught about the gods and learned to respect them. This boy is being taught rhetoric – the art of public speaking – by his tutor.

MORNINGS WITH THE GODS

Every morning Romans made offerings to their household gods, as Hindu families do today. After breakfast, the son of this family gets ready to walk to school with his slave. His sister will stay at home with her mother and learn the skills of running a large household.

GODS WHO CARED

Aesculapius God of medicine (left, with Hygeia)

Bonus Eventus God who brought success in enterprises and made things turn out for the best

Deverra Spirit of the broom (for sweeping clean)

Fortuna Goddess of chance, who could tell the future

Hygeia Goddess of health; the daughter (sometimes wife) of Aesculapius

Hymen God of marriage

Orbona Goddess who looked after orphans

Pilumnus and Picumnus Twin gods who looked after new-born babies

Terminus God who watched over property

Viriplace God who soothed quarrels between wife and husband

▼ This family altar from Pompeii shows two household gods dancing on either side of the master of the house. The snake below symbolizes the Genius of the house.

JUPITER AND JUNO

JUPITER WAS ruler of the universe. This great sky god did exactly as he pleased. He created storms and lightning and hurled thunderbolts in anger. People had every reason to fear him and hold him in awe.

Jupiter was also a warrior god, who inspired Rome's army. After winning battles, generals offered Jupiter a gold crown of victory. Each year the Romans held Games in his honour, including running and chariot races.

JUNO'S SACRED GEESE

Sacred geese kept at Juno's temple on the Capitol (the centre of Rome) once saved Rome from its enemies. When invading Gauls tried to climb the walls of the citadel, the geese's cackling warned Rome's defenders in time to drive off the attack.

FARMER'S LIFE

Most Romans were farmers. They relied on the soil and the weather, so they took pains never to anger Jupiter since he controlled the sun, wind, rain and everything that affected their lives. The Romans grew corn for making bread, olives for making oil, and grapes for making wine. Slaves worked

▲ A bust of Juno from Rome. Our month of June is named after her. Juno was usually shown with her peacock, Argus, by her side.

◄ Jupiter, the chief Roman god, stands at his altar. The eagle at his feet represents his power.

the fields for their master landowners. Sudden rainstorms caused by Jupiter's wrath could ruin the harvest.

JUNO, SISTER AND WIFE

Juno was Jupiter's sister as well as his wife. She was a mother goddess, who looked after women, marriage and childbirth. As the ideal woman, she became the symbol of the perfect Roman wife and mother. But Juno's husband was not perfect, and the goddess had many rivals for his affections. In fits of jealous rage, Juno often took revenge on them. Jupiter and Juno, together with Jupiter's favourite daughter, Minerva (see page 22), were among Rome's most important gods.

JUPITER'S SACRED COW

Jupiter used all kinds of tricks to stop his wife finding out about his adventures. To avoid his wife attacking Io, a nymph (see page 23) with whom he had fallen in love, Jupiter turned the girl into a beautiful white cow. This 17th-century painting shows Jupiter presenting the transformed nymph to his wife. The largest moon of the planet Jupiter is named after Io.

NEPTUNE, GOD OF THE SEA

THE GOD Neptune shared with his brothers the wealth of their father, Saturn. Jupiter won the earth, Pluto the underworld and Neptune the sea. Neptune in his palace beneath the waves had total power over the sea and those who sailed on it. With his weapon, the trident, he could raise storms or calm the raging waves. When angry he could cause shipwrecks, split rocks and create earthquakes.

The Romans depended on the sea for fishing and trading, and for transporting troops. Sea travel was dangerous. Sailors, traders and fishermen prayed to Neptune to keep them safe, and visited his shrine to give thanks when they returned safe home.

In the hot Italian summer, the Romans celebrated the festival of Neptune, who was also

AENEAS AND THE STORM

The poet Virgil told this story about Aeneas, a hero who had angered the goddess Juno. When Aeneas set sail with his fleet, Juno rushed to the wind god Aeolus in his underwater cave. She begged him for a storm to kill Aeneas. In return she offered him a beautiful sea nymph. Aeolus at once set free his four winds (below). They churned up the waves and shattered the ships, tossing masts, beams and sailors overboard like sticks of wood. Aeneas prayed, but the gods seemed deaf. Then Neptune in his ocean depths noticed wreckage and bodies sinking to the sea bed. He recognized the wicked work of Juno. Furious, he called the winds to cease. Then, riding over the waters, he calmed them so that Aeneas could sail on with what was left of his fleet.

▲ Tritons, nereids (sea nymphs) and a sea-antelope are pictured on this Roman mosaic. Tritons were descendants of Neptune's son. The Romans believed these mermen caused shipwrecks and other mishaps.

▲ A merman (half man, half fish) is pictured on this ancient pot. Neptune's son Triton was a merman.

AT NEPTUNE'S MERCY

Neptune's symbol of power was a trident, a three-pronged spear, used by Roman fishermen. His goodwill was vital to them. As well as small fishing boats, the Romans had wide sailing ships for carrying goods, and ships called galleys for transporting troops or fighting battles. Sea travel was rarely undertaken during winter for fear of Neptune's storms.

god of freshwater rivers, lakes and streams. Farmers needed the god's help to keep water flowing for their ripening crops.

NEPTUNE'S FAMILY

Neptune and his wife, the sea nymph Amphitrite, had a son called Triton who was half man, half fish. He acted as a messenger and herald for his father, blowing on a conch shell to stir up the waters or calm them. When a human hornplayer called Misenus challenged his skill, Triton caused him to drown.

◀ Neptune rode the seas in a horse-drawn chariot, attended by dolphins. He was god of horses as well as the sea, and father of the famous winged horse, Pegasus.

PLUTO AND THE UNDERWORLD

THE ROMANS believed that when they died they would go to the underworld which was deep in the centre of the earth. It was reached through openings such as caves or deep lakes. King of the underworld was Pluto, brother of Jupiter. He had a thick beard and held a black sceptre and fork. People found him gloomy but not frightening. He was linked to cypress trees, which are a symbol of grief and often grown in Italian graveyards.

ORPHEUS AND EURYDICE

The Romans loved this old Greek story. Orpheus was a miraculous musician. He sang and played the lyre so sweetly that animals followed him, and rivers became still to listen. When his wife Eurydice died, Orpheus followed her soul to the underworld. His music so charmed Pluto and Proserpina that they agreed to let Eurydice return to life and daylight, on condition that Orpheus did not look back on the upward journey. The pair set off, but Orpheus could not resist a backward glance. As he did so, Eurydice vanished and was lost to him for ever.

CERES AND PROSERPINA

Pluto was so ugly that he could find no girl willing to be his wife. So he captured Proserpina, the beautiful daughter of Ceres, the goddess of corn

▼ This Roman floor mosaic shows Orpheus charming the beasts.

ROMAN FUNERALS

When a Roman citizen died, his wife would let her hair hang loose as a sign of grief. Slaves would wait for the man's will to be read, for it was the custom for some slaves to be freed when their master died. At the funeral, these ex-slaves carried his body on an

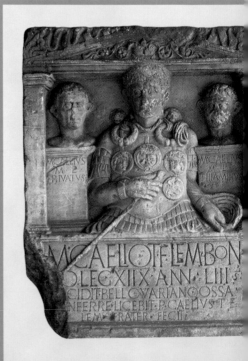

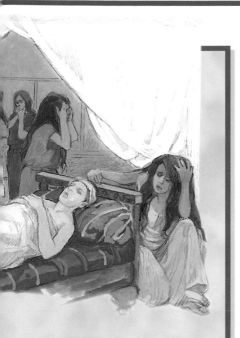

open bier. Priests led the funeral procession and prayers. Musicians played mournful music and women wailed. A member of the family made a speech in praise of the man. Then he was buried in a tomb outside the town. The picture in the panel (below left) shows the tombstone of a centurion and two freed slaves.

PEOPLE AND PLACES OF THE DEAD

Genii Protective spirits who escorted the dead on their journey through the afterlife.

Hell The place where wicked people are punished after death.

Lake Avernus near Pozzuoli had links to the underworld. Its wooded hills were pitted with caverns, through which (so it was believed) the dead could be summoned.

Lemures Mischievous ghosts who came back from the dead to torment the living.

Orcus God of death (often confused with Pluto) carried off people by force.

and plenty, and carried her off to his underground kingdom.

Ceres looked everywhere for her lost daughter. Finally she gave up hope of finding her on earth and lit a torch to light her way into the darkness of the underworld. There she pleaded with Pluto and threatened to destroy the world by famine. But Pluto would not give up his bride. So Ceres carried out her threat. She caused a drought so severe that everywhere farm crops withered in the sun. Nothing would grow.

To prevent disaster Jupiter had to act. He ruled that Proserpina should stay above ground with Ceres for six months, and return to live with Pluto for the other six. For the Romans, this myth explained the changing of the seasons, from the bright days of summer to the gloom of winter.

▲ An ancient tomb painting showing a dead soul being escorted to the underworld by genii.

MARS AND VULCAN

FIGHTING WAS a way of life for the Romans. They marched across Europe, defeating hostile tribes and making them part of their empire. Roman generals and their troops trusted in the gods to bring them victory and they did so almost unfailingly.

MARS AND VENUS

Mars showed the gentler side to his nature when he fell in love with Venus, the goddess of love and beauty. She alone was able to subdue his warlike temper. Cupid was their son. But like some of the other gods, Mars found it difficult to remain faithful. He fell in love with at least two Vestal Virgins, persuading them to forget their vows. One of them, Rhea Silvia, gave birth to his two sons – Romulus and Remus (see page 4). This wall painting (below) from Pompeii shows Mars and Venus at home with their son Cupid.

MARS, GOD OF WAR

Mars was the son of Juno, and father of Romulus and Remus. After Jupiter, he was the Romans' most important god. The first month of the old Roman year was March. It marked the beginning of spring and was dedicated to Mars because in the old days, when the Romans were simple farmers, he was their god of fertility and farming. As the Romans moved from farming to empire-building, they made

▲ Roman soldiers looked to Mars to bring them victory in war.

▼ A bronze statue of the fiery god Vulcan. His anger was made worse by his wife Venus who was often unfaithful to him.

Roman soldiers were well armed and well trained. When the army was on the move, the foot soldiers marched 30 kilometres or more in a day, carrying all their kit and rations. Discipline could be harsh but there were honours and rewards. Retired soldiers were often given land to farm. The Romans honoured Mars with Games where they competed in warlike sports and horse races.

their favourite Mars into their god of war, which was now their main concern.

VULCAN, THE FIERY BLACKSMITH

Vulcan was god of fire, metalworking and craftsmanship. He was the blacksmith of the gods, hammering armour and weapons, some of them magical. He made Jupiter's thunderbolts and could start and control the spread of fire. Vulcan's forge was under Mount Etna, the volcano on the island of Sicily.

To punish Venus, goddess of love, for her pride, Jupiter made her marry the fiery Vulcan who was lame and ugly. On Vulcan's chief festival day, the Romans threw offerings of fish into a sacred fire, perhaps because water creatures were normally beyond the god's reach.

◄ This statue shows Mars as strong and powerful. Tuesday was his day, as we are reminded by its French name of Mardi.

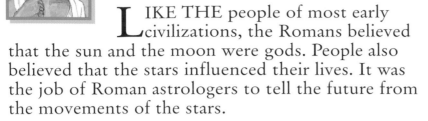

APOLLO AND DIANA

LIKE THE people of most early civilizations, the Romans believed that the sun and the moon were gods. People also believed that the stars influenced their lives. It was the job of Roman astrologers to tell the future from the movements of the stars.

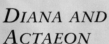

APOLLO, THE SUN GOD

Apollo was one of Jupiter's many children. A famous Greek story told how, as a four-day-old baby, Apollo fought and killed the serpent-monster Python, which had tried to kill his mother Leto.

Apollo left the realm of the gods and for many years roamed the world, slaying giants with his arrows and even challenging the mighty Hercules (see page 26). Jupiter had to make peace between the two warriors.

Perhaps to keep his son out of further trouble, Jupiter gave him the task of spreading light across

DIANA AND ACTAEON

Diana's beauty attracted hopeful lovers, but she would have none of them. A famous story told how she was pursued by the hunter Actaeon. In her anger, the goddess turned him into a stag, which was then pursued and killed by Actaeon's own hounds. This detail from a mosaic floor shows Diana hunting, riding on a stag.

▲ This is a Roman copy of a Greek head of Apollo. The Romans thought Apollo was the 'ideal' young man.

▶ This sculpture shows Diana the huntress fastening her robe.

▼ Apollo stands with the centaur Chiron and the Greek doctor Hippocrates in this wall painting from Pompeii.

FEAST OF DIANA

Diana was the protector of the lower classes. Her festival on 13 August was a holiday for Roman slaves who held merry celebrations in her honour. They gathered near the steps of her temple to drink and dance into the night.

the world. In a chariot made by Vulcan, Apollo drove the sun across the sky each day from dawn to dusk.

Apollo enjoyed eternal youth and had many love affairs. He chased Daphne, a maiden from Thessaly, until she turned into a laurel bush in order to escape him. To attract the nymph Driope, the god took the form of a tortoise.

As well as being the god of light, Apollo was also god of medicine, archery, poetry, arts and music. He played a lyre, a stringed instrument invented by his little brother Mercury. He was also a shepherd-god, protecting flocks.

DIANA, GODDESS OF THE MOON

Diana was Apollo's twin sister and goddess of the moon. She flew across the heavens in a chariot drawn by a flock of doves. On earth, Diana was the goddess of woods and the hunt. She was often shown with a bow and quiver, and accompanied by a hound or a deer.

Diana was so beautiful that many gods and mortals fell in love with her, but she rejected them all. Even so, women who wanted to have babies said special prayers to her.

MERCURY AND MINERVA

T HE ROMANS brought law and order – and peace – to the world. This encouraged trade, for traders could move their goods around without fear of robbers or pirates. The god of trade was Mercury, but he was also god of thieves.

MERCURY, MESSENGER OF THE GODS

Mercury was another of Jupiter's sons. He was the winged messenger of the gods, a small, clever, cunning individual who was a jack-of-all-trades. He was god not just of traders and thieves, but also of gamblers, orators, travellers, merchants and industry. He was shown holding a purse full of money and had a salesperson's easy way with words. He was always ready to help and always on the move.

One of Mercury's roles was to guide adventurers and travellers. Some say he led the souls of the dead to the underworld. His magic powers and unearthly

▲ This bronze bust of Minerva shows her wearing her helmet. Above all the other gods, she was credited with tactical skill in warfare.

MERCURY'S WINNING WAYS

When he was just one day old, Mercury showed his cleverness by making a lyre for his brother Apollo. He then displayed his criminal side, by stealing Apollo's oxen. Apollo took him to Jupiter for a telling-off, but little Mercury got off lightly. He played the lyre so beautifully that Jupiter's anger turned to pleasure at his son's brilliance. He gave Mercury a winged cap, winged shoes and the job of gods' messenger.

MERCHANTS

Goods brought in from the countryside or made in workshops were sold in Rome's shops and markets. Traders used scales to weigh goods, and standards were strictly enforced. Weights and measures, and the values of coins, were the same throughout the empire. People carried their money in small leather pouches, just like Mercury.

speed made him a useful friend. The French keep his name in Mercredi (Wednesday).

MINERVA, GODDESS OF WISDOM

Minerva was one of the greatest goddesses. She was goddess of wisdom and good advice, the art of warfare, science, all arts and skills, especially weaving and spinning. She was the patron of cobblers, carpenters, artists, poets, doctors and schools. People believed that anything she promised would come about. Her shrine was a meeting place for craftsmen, poets and actors.

Minerva was often shown wearing a helmet and holding a spear and a magic shield. Sometimes she held a distaff (used for spinning), and sometimes the twig of an olive tree. Her animals, the owl and the cock, were always near her.

▲ This small statue of Mercury shows him carrying his purse and his caduceus. This rod with two snakes coiled about it symbolized his importance as a sacred messenger.

MERCURY AND ARGUS

Mercury was always ready to lend a hand with his father's love affairs. Jupiter loved Io and had turned the beautiful girl into a cow in order to deceive his wife. He gave the beast to Juno but she was not fooled and kept the cow well guarded by a 100-eyed man named Argus. Mercury slew Argus, whose eyes were transferred by Juno to the tail of the peacock. In his version of the legend the painter Rubens shows Mercury lulling Argus to sleep with his flute so that he can cut off his head and steal the cow away.

VENUS AND CUPID

ROMANTIC LOVE played little official part in the life of most Romans. Juno presided over marriage. In patrician (upper class) families, daughters might be only twelve when they married and take no part in choosing their husband. Plebeians (working class people) had more freedom but little time for romance, while slaves were too busy working. But love finds a way, and in Rome its way was led by Venus and her son Cupid.

CUPID AND PSYCHE

Psyche was a princess who was so beautiful that Venus was mad with jealousy. In her fury, she told Cupid to make Psyche fall in love with the ugliest man in the world. Unfortunately, when Cupid saw Psyche he scratched himself with one of his own arrows, and promptly fell in love with her himself. To avoid upsetting his mother, he visited Psyche only at night and told her that she must never see him in the light. But Psyche disobeyed him and lit a lamp to snatch a glimpse of him. At once, he deserted her, leaving her to wander the world trying to find him. Spiteful Venus did her best to make Psyche's plight more miserable. But in the end soft-hearted Jupiter took pity on the poor girl. He granted her immortality, and she and Cupid were reunited. This 15th-century picture shows episodes from the story.

VENUS, GODDESS OF LOVE AND BEAUTY

Venus was at first goddess of gardens. She was especially important to the Romans, who believed she was mother of the whole human race. Venus was

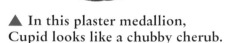

▶ This little statue of Venus shows her crowned and carrying the apple she won as the prize in the beauty contest judged by the hero Paris.

▲ In this plaster medallion, Cupid looks like a chubby cherub.

famous for her beauty. In a beauty contest judged by Paris, Prince of Troy, she defeated both Juno and Minerva to win the prize. Venus is usually shown as a young, smiling girl. The goddess was the wife of Vulcan, but Mars probably was the father of her son, although in some stories Jupiter or Mercury is his father.

CUPID, GOD OF LOVE
Cupid was a playful lad with a bow and arrows. His arrows were full of passion and whoever was struck by them fell in love. In statues, the Romans made him a naked, winged boy (rather like a cherub).

The little love-god was also blindfolded, to show that 'love is blind' and that Cupid shot his love-darts without knowing whom they might hit. The Romans carved pictures of him (often asleep or drunk) on tombstones, to represent the pleasant sleep of death.

A WEDDING
On her wedding day, a Roman bride was led to her new home by torchbearers and musicians. Three friends of the bridegroom would carry her over the threshhold so that her feet would not touch the ground.

CERES AND COUNTRY GODS

THE ROMANS were, first of all, farmers and shepherds. They believed in a great many spirits of nature, some wild and mischievous, others generous and helpful. Even when they ruled a vast empire and many people lived in cities, they still felt attached to the simple, country life. Many patricians had country estates, and retired soldiers were rewarded with country properties.

GOD OF FLOCKS

Faunus was half goat and half man, a wild god of the hills and the flocks of animals that roamed them. Like the shepherds who tended their flocks on the hillsides, Faunus played panpipes, an instrument named after the Greek god Pan. The pipes were said to have been invented by the nymph Syrinx, who escaped the god's unwanted attentions only by turning herself into a clump of reeds.

FAUNUS AND HERCULES

Faunus was always eager to try his luck with girls. One story told how he surprised Hercules and his beloved asleep on a moonless night. Unbeknown to Faunus, the two humans had swopped clothes. Faunus whispered sweet nothings in the ear of the sleeping 'girl', until the muscular Hercules awoke and sent him packing! After this, to avoid confusion, Faunus insisted his priests wear no clothes. The Romans kept up the tradition in the Lupercalia, a festival celebrated on 15 February, when even noble Romans could be found enjoying themselves in the streets naked save for a goatskin.

WATCHING THE FLOCKS

Only wealthy Romans regularly ate meat, but everybody had ewe's or goat's milk and cheese. Landowners kept flocks of sheep and goats that were

▼ This wall painting from Naples shows Flora stripping blooms as she passes.

▼ In this 19th-century German painting, two fauns watch a sleeping nymph. The Romans believed that a whole race of creatures who were half man, half goat lived in the countryside.

GODS OF FRUITFUL HARVESTS

The Romans had many other country gods, some of them very old, others borrowed from the Greeks. Nearly all had to do with the farming year. Ceres taught people to plough, sow, reap and bake. She was usually shown carrying a sheaf of corn, as a symbol of fruitfulness. She was also pictured searching for her lost daughter Proserpina (see page 16).

Flora was the goddess of springtime, of vines, fruit trees and flowers. Her companion, Pomona, also helped watch over the orchards. Spring festivals to celebrate Flora had a reputation for bawdiness and the blossoming of romances.

guarded mostly by young boys. To pass the time these young herdsmen played tunes on delicate pipes made from hollowed-out reeds. They used the pipes to help round up the animals for milking.

ECHO AND NARCISSUS

The Roman poet Ovid told this story in his collection of tales Metamorphoses. *It is from an old Greek legend. A handsome youth named Narcissus was so in love with himself that he rejected all the girls who fell for him, including the nymph Echo. The gods were angry and condemned Narcissus to gaze at his own reflection in a pond until he wasted away and died. Only a flower remained, the narcissus. Poor Echo pined for her lost love, and she became just an unseen voice in the rocks and trees. In this painting by Poussin, Narcissus gazes at his reflection while Echo watches from a rock with a love never to be returned.*

BACCHUS AND HIS REVELS

BACCHUS, another son of Jupiter, was the Roman god of wine. His mother was not a goddess but a human called Semele. The wine god was a handsome young man. Pictures show him riding on a wine barrel, crowned with garlands of vine leaves and grapes, and carrying a goblet. Often he rides in a chariot drawn by leopards. Sometimes he has two horns as a symbol of his power.

BACCHUS AND THE PIRATES

Bacchus had many adventures on his travels. Once he was captured by sea pirates who bound him with thick ropes. But the knots came undone on their own. The sea around the pirate ship turned to wine, and a green vine grew up its mast. Bacchus changed into a roaring lion, and all the pirates, save one, leaped overboard, and were turned into dolphins. One sailor who was spared guided Bacchus to the island of Naxos, where he met his wife-to-be, Ariadne.

▲ Roman wall painting of Bacchus and one of his followers. His coronet is made of vine leaves and flowers.

◀ This famous painting by Caravaggio shows Bacchus crowned with grapes and vine leaves.

▲ A pre-Roman vase shows the head of a faun and a maenad, typical followers of the god Bacchus.

Bacchus had the gift of prophecy, and could assume animal shape. He taught humans to plant grapevines and to make wine, and travelled far to spread the knowledge. For this he became a god himself. He married Ariadne, a Cretan princess.

DRUNKEN REVELS

Bacchus is almost never alone. He is followed first by his friend and tutor Silenus, who was the son of Faunus (see page 26). Then come nymphs, other fauns, shepherds and female revellers called maenads. This throng of followers are always drunkenly singing, dancing and enjoying themselves.

▲ In this Roman sculpture, followers of Bacchus bring wine and food to the festivities. Most of his fans were women.

PARTY TIME

Wine played an important part in Roman life and making it was hard work. Slaves trod the grapes with bare feet, dancing on them rhythmically to the sound of pipes and drums. Once made, the new wine was tasted and everyone gave thanks to Bacchus. Each year the Romans held a festival in his honour. It was called the Bacchanalia and was an excuse for drunkenness and wild behaviour, which is the meaning of the word 'bacchanalian'.

GLOSSARY

Aeneas Hero of Roman and Greek stories. His adventures were told in a long poem, the *Aeneid*, by Virgil.

altar Table used for offering up sacrifices.

astrologer Person who studies the supposed effects of the stars on people's lives and actions.

augur Roman who foretold the future from omens.

bier Frame, like a stretcher, on which a dead person is carried to the grave.

brazier Basket or tray holding hot coals.

bronze Metal alloy made from copper and tin.

bust Sculpture of a person's head, shoulders and chest.

caduceus Mercury's rod, a wand with two wings on top and two serpents twined round it.

centaur Creature that was half man, half horse.

centurion Commander of 100 men in the Roman army.

chariot Wheeled carriage pulled by horses, used in Roman times for racing or in battle.

citadel Fortress in or near a city.

citizen Person living in a city. Roman citizens, but not slaves, had special rights and privileges.

cobbler Shoemender.

conch Shell used as a trumpet by the Tritons.

coronet Small crown or headdress.

curse To wish evil on someone.

cypress Cone-bearing tree whose branches were carried at funerals and so it became a symbol of death.

distaff Stick that holds a tuft of wool or flax when someone is spinning.

entrails Insides of an animal.

famine Lack of food, affecting a number of people.

faun Creature with a man's head and body, and a goat's horns, hind legs and tail.

fertility Fruitfulness, producing plenty.

forum Public meeting- or market-place, especially the Forum in Rome.

garland Necklace or circle of flowers.

genius Spirit of good or evil that accompanied people; plural is genii.

goblet Large drinking cup without a handle.

god Supernatural being who is worshipped.

hearth Place in a house where the fire is lit.

Hercules (Greek Herakles) In Greek myth, hero famous for his strength.

Hippocrates (died about 370BC) Greek physician, known as the father of medicine.

incense Substance burned to give off perfumed smoke, especially during a religious ceremony.

lot Item, such as a long or short straw, drawn in a lottery to decide, for example, who will get a particular task or prize.

lyre Musical instrument like a harp, used to accompany poetry.

maenad Woman follower of the wine-god Bacchus.

muse One of nine daughters of Jupiter, who inspired poetry, music and other arts.

nereid Sea, or water, nymphs.

nymph Spirit living in mountains, seas, rivers, trees and woodland; young and beautiful girl-like creatures.

omen Sign of a future event, either good or bad.

oratory Art of speaking to an audience, studied in Roman times.

Ovid Roman poet (43BC-AD17?) His poem *Metamorphoses* describes the adventures and love affairs of gods and heroes.

Paris Prince of Troy. He judged a beauty contest between Venus, Juno and Minerva, and he stole away the Greek princess Helen and so caused the Trojan War.

patrician Person belonging to one of the first families of Rome, an aristocrat of the early Roman Republic.

Pegasus Winged horse, the offspring of Poseidon and the Gorgon Medusa.

plebeian Common people of early Roman Republic; freed slaves, peasants and farmers.

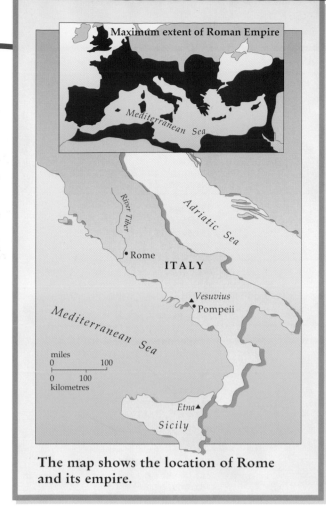

Maximum extent of Roman Empire

The map shows the location of Rome and its empire.

ROMAN GOD = GREEK GOD

AESCULAPIUS	ASKLEPIOS
APOLLO	APOLLO
BACCHUS	DIONYSOS
CERES	DEMETER
CUPID	EROS
DIANA	ARTEMIS
FAUNUS	PAN
JUNO	HERA
JUPITER	ZEUS
MARS	ARES
MERCURY	HERMES
MINERVA	ATHENA
NEPTUNE	POSEIDON
PLUTO	HADES
SATURN	KRONOS
VENUS	APHRODITE
VESTA	HESTIA
VULCAN	HEPHAISTOS

Pompeii Ancient city in Italy, destroyed and buried in ash by the volcano Vesuvius in AD79.

priest/priestess Person with special religious duties.

quiver Pouch in which an archer carries arrows.

religion System of beliefs involving the worship of supernatural powers, identified as gods and goddesses.

ritual Set actions (words, music, offerings) performed as part of religious worship.

sacred Special or holy in a religious sense.

sacrifice Offerings made to a god, such as food and drink, and particularly an animal killed for the purpose.

sheaf Bundle of wheat stalks gathered and bound together at harvest time.

shrine Place with special religious meaning, usually with a small statue of a god or goddess.

soothsayer Person believed to foretell, or divine, the future.

spirit Part of a person independent of the body; also a supernatural being, sometimes without a body, but also believed to take human and animal forms.

temple Building set aside for religious worship.

Tiber River in Italy on which Rome stands.

trident Three-pronged fork, used to spear fish and as a weapon by gladiators in the Roman arena.

tutor Teacher, often one hired to teach pupils one-to-one.

underworld Place in which the spirits of the dead dwell.

Vestal Virgin Unmarried woman dedicated to looking after the sacred flame of the goddess Vesta.

vines Plants on which grapes grow.

Virgil (Publius Vergilius Maro 70-19BC) Greatest Roman poet, who wrote the epic *Aeneid* and poems about country life.